TRUE BELIEVER

"If you ever wondered what a villanelle about supervillains would look like, then face front and read *True Believer*. Kass's collection of Marvel-themed poetry is obsessive and witty—I regret only that he didn't find a rhyme for 'Excelsior'!"

—Gavin Edwards, coauthor of the *New York Times* bestseller
MCU: The Reign of Marvel Studios

"*True Believer* is Jeff Kass at his best: reflective and clobbery, nerdy and dynamic, witty and wise. In these poems history meets myth, the epic intertwines with the intimate, and nostalgia joins forces with imagination to seek out justice. Best of all, Jeff is clearly having fun here, and you will too."

—Adam Mansbach, *New York Times* bestselling author of
Go the F*ck to Sleep and *The Golem of Brooklyn*

"These are glimmering poems that tackle the heroic, the collective, the comic, the intimate, the fantastical, the daily, the strange. I read this book cover-to-cover."

—Carlina Duan, author of *Alien Miss*

"In a world where problems can feel insurmountable, *True Believer* reminds us that no gift is too small to make a mark; reminds us that there's a hero in us all if we can find a way to trust in ourselves and each other."

—Lauren Whitehead, writer, performer, professor at NYU
Tisch School of the Arts

Kass will smash! In this clever, wise, and dare I say *fun* collection your soon-to-be-favorite poet-storyteller smashes Marvel superheroes against Jewish folklore against systemic American violence against masculinity—all with earnest grace. I turned these pages expecting to see love donning a cape and washboard abs as it pulled the wounded from a burning building. Instead, I walk away feeling that love is how any one of us, at any moment, might rise into a private, extraordinary courage."

—Shira Erlichman, author of *Odes to Lithium*

"Jeff Kass is a *True Believer*—and true believers know: the line between worlds is thin. These poems are love songs: to the hulking, colorful heroes of comic book lore, and to the plain-clothed Avengers among us—committed teachers, leaf blowers, cab drivers, tired parents, baseball coaches. But in true Kass form, these odes also whisper the gentlest kind of dare: But what's *your* origin story, friend?"

—Adam Falkner, author *The Willies*

"Jeff Kass's new collection uses the motif of the comic book hero and villain to ask the eternal questions of human experience. These poems are not the cardboard creations of an entertainment industry bereft of new ideas but rather they embody the thing that a great comic can: using the familiar structures of a well-trod story to interrogate the themes that animate us all. In particular, the long poems show a virtuosity in which the writer marries personal experience, comic book lore, biography, and history to open up new imaginative landscapes. These are poems worth their weight in Vibranium."

—Nate Marshall, author *Finna* and *Wild Hundreds*

TRUE
BELIEVER

POEMS

JEFF KASS

DZANC
BOOKS

DZANC
BOOKS

2580 Craig Rd.
Ann Arbor, MI 48103
www.dzancbooks.org

First Edition: March 2025
Cover design by Matthew Revert
Interior design by Michelle Dotter

ISBN: 9781938603266

Notes:
Lyrics to Redbone's "Come and Get Your Love" by Lolly Vegas
Lyrics to Led Zeppelin's "Immigrant Song" by Robert Plant
"Face it, Tiger, you just hit the jackpot," spoken by Mary Jane Watson in *Amazing Spider-Man* #42, written by Stan Lee
Tales of Suspense # 80, "He Who Holds the Cosmic Cube," written by Stan Lee
"Panther's Rage" Black Panther sequence written by Don McGregor with Stan Lee
Lyrics to "Danny's Song" by Kenny Loggins

Printed in the United States of America

10   9   8   7   6   5   4   3   2   1

CONTENTS

I.

ELEGY FOR STAN LEE

I think I always knew I'd never be a hero.

Not, at least, the kind who scuttled up
the sides of buildings, or zinged explosive-
tipped arrows through the rib of a gas tank
two miles distant. I'd never be able to transform
into a flying blaze or conjure ice bridges
from my fingertips. Never use my built-in
radar-sense to read the sound of a pistol's hammer-
click in a hurricane, or windmill an adamantium
shield through the hate-filled heart of a hostile spaceship,
then boomerang it back mid-backflip to my vise-grip.

But I had my own Kingpins, my own
Red Skulls, Dr. Dooms, and Doc Ocks.

They looked like the kid twice my size
who slung-shot a thumbtack half a centimeter
from my left eye. They looked like a yawning
Friday night when nobody called to see if I wanted
to go to a movie, like my inability to ice skate
with any alacrity, like mountains of worksheets
in chemistry, like the kid with the confectionery
golf swing who swung up in a Toyota Celica
and swooped up the girl I was too afraid to talk to.

No, I never thought I'd be lucky enough to be bitten

by a radioactive spider, zapped by a Gamma ray,
or win the cosmic lottery and be born a mutant.

Yet, I *was* born a mutant.

Wasn't I?

Somewhere, nestled in my unique DNA,
latent like magma bubbling in the dark-lit
realm of the Mole Man, does there not lurk
a fiery force?

Even if it couldn't help me launch a baseball over a fence,
or elbow-dunk above the gymnasium rim, or grow six
inches taller, or earn an A in calculus, or somehow
convince that girl I was someone worth flirting
with, still—

there's *something* inside me, right?

Think of it—a boy, ten years old,
like so many millions of others,
horizontal on his bedroom carpet,
elbows propped on the floor, chin
braced in his hands and spread out
before him—

four
gigantic
block
letters

slightly slanted
usually red
outlined in black

T-H-O-R

God of Thunder!

mockingly called Goldilocks
by the wisecracking Hawkeye

spinning his mighty hammer through the cosmos
so he can battle the Enchantress, the Executioner,
Namor, or that other four-lettered creature, the great
green behemoth who can scoop up a city bus and throw
it in a perfect spiral the length of a football field—

what a riveting, heartbreaking, titanic, hulk-
of-a-narrative tucked into twenty tactile
and colorful newspaper-print pages

for that boy

bored on a rainy
February Sunday

that boy

dreaming of greatness
in the heavy heat of August

that boy

learning the lifelong weight
of failing to stop a thief
who will later that very night
murder the beloved uncle

learning the shame of a man terrified
even a blind woman can't love his rocky
skin

learning to live a code that says
teamwork, keeping one's smack-
talking cool in a crisis and a never,
never, never-say-die spirit can defeat

The Rhino

The Juggernaut

The Toad

The Lizard

The Vulture

The Blob

even that horrific
magenta world-
swallower

Galactus!

what power for that boy
who wants to believe
in essential goodness

wants to believe whatever lesson
he plans for his sophomores will be
epic, whatever practice he plans
for his son's baseball team will be
monumental, whatever sandwich
he concocts can ward off the rankest
evil, whatever kiss he tenders his wife
will un-snap Thanos's fingers
and save the universe.

That faith in his own potential
is embedded in his brain,
has clamored there half-
a-century.

It's clobberin' time!

Flame on!

GHAZAL FOR ANYONE WHO WANTS TO BE A MARVEL SUPERHERO

Get a job. Sell your baseball cards. If you have a fur coat, hock it.
Fighting crime doesn't pay either, you'll need cash in your pocket.

Be prepared to meet astounding creatures—a mutant coiled in steel,
a villain with a condominium-sized head, a talking raccoon, Rocket.

If you encounter a meteor laced with poison plunging toward
a hospital, stop it. You cannot run and hide. Curl your fist, sock it.

If a portal to another universe opens, don't be tempted to explore
destinies elsewhere, slam that door shut. If possible, lock it.

You may have to tangle with a wacko named Electro. His
impolite behavior may shock you, like a fork in a socket.

Most likely, you'll need to forget about love. It's too dangerous,
best store the memory of intimacy 'round your neck in a locket.

You'll sport a cool costume that shows off your corded muscles,
your checkerboard abs. It's good promo for heroes, rock it.

It ain't an easy existence, the Thing'll tell ya, but with persistence, you'll
save many lives, maybe a hack poet will write about you, don't knock it.

DAREDEVIL CREED

I believe in what the eyes cannot see, the rumble
        of a truck four blocks away, its thick tires
        splashing through puddles, a bookie
        with a broken clavicle rope-tied in the back,
        blood gurgling from his lips, the driver,
        equipped with a bruising baseball bat,
        about to dump him into the East River.

I believe in the scent of the cigar the driver's smoking,
        a smell I've smelled before, three days ago, when
        he walked into Sammy's Deli to order a corned beef
        on rye with Russian dressing, not a Reuben, *no sauer-*
        kraut, the counter man said, *but toasted, right, Albert?*

        The driver is Albert.

I believe in swinging off the roof of this building,
        hurling the hook from my billy-club
        into space and trusting it will snag a fire
        escape. I will bolt from my perch by
        the abandoned water tower and meet
        the truck at the wharf before the bookie
        splashes into the river's dark.

        I am a man with no eyes
        and slashing fists
        that do not miss.

I believe my punches pack the power of my dead father.
　　Albert, I will say, this bookie is no saint. He too
　　has beaten people bloody. The confessions remain
　　on his tongue. He muttered them along with prayers
　　for a miracle in the back of your truck. Albert, I am
　　that miracle.

Albert, there's no use hiding from the truth. You are
　　not a man without fear. One day, you will need
　　saving too. You will breathe your own confession
　　at the point of a gun and pray the man with no eyes
　　will descend from the rooftops, a Gabriel falling
　　to your rescue.

OUTSIDE SCHOOL TODAY

Workers in neon vests circle in clumps
like ants around a discarded pizza
crust. Out here, in the real world

these men and women who clutch
thermoses of steaming coffee
to their chests and gather to discuss
what needs be done with the trench
dug adjacent to the Earth Science
greenhouse, or buzz along on a lawn-
mower across the JV soccer field are,
perhaps, who my students will become
whence they peel their plum-colored
vestments of commencement.

Let's be honest, nobody honors these neon-
skinned workers as warriors, but think
of Thanos, most powerful being
in history, wielder of a gauntlet
jeweled with infinity.

When the Avengers find him,
what is he doing if not watering
his garden, as if the reason half
the universe had to vamoose was
too many of us are unwilling
to plunge our hands into dirt.

What kind of supercilious jerk am I
to hope my students will grow into
architects of addictive algorithms,
or crafters of crypto-empires, and not
wielders of leaf-blowers, breathers
of gasoline and carcinogenic dust?

Let's, again, be honest. We are all extras
in this story, anonymous bags of bones
snuffed and vaporized when the multi-
verse ruptures and gargantuan battleships
shaped like steel-plated truck tires crunch
the skeins of our fragile frames.

Oh, woman in neon T-shirt, camouflage
ballcap, sunglasses shining as if you are
a fighter pilot swerving your earthmover
past the woodchip-filled garden
and entrance to E-hall, if the great rolling
spaceship were to flatten you, know I witnessed
you conducting your grand machine, mastering
the wheels beneath as you slurped up dirt
and relocated it from one place to another.

Know if you were the one inhabiting
Iron Man's tricked-out suit of armor
your fist too could pulverize the Bobcat
you pilot.

Avengers, Assemble! I shout
to my students, *time to return
to the classroom,* share
the poems we've written

that commemorate this day
on which we are not yet
overrun.

STAR-LORD'S DANCE

If you're Star-Lord, you don't even balk, man
You just flick the switch on the Sony Walkman
The planet hisses dark, slimy, grimy like inside a sewer
But that *Hail, Hail,* hits like an instant spirit-renewer
You're kicking lizards with every footfall
Don't hesitate, just boot 'em like a football
Field goal, watch 'em soar through the uprights
You spin and half-step, fist-rep in every rough fight
Trolls brand you the ugliest Chris on the internet
But you just keep on grooving, ain't been hindered yet
Clowns claim you're a better raggedy Andy on *Parks n Rec*
But you stay cosmic looking for apocalyptic schemes to wreck
Your mother's music echoes through your dometop
The kind of souvenir you can't get when you home-shop
Hail, Hail and you spread your arms wide, gyrate like a stoned top
A Hanukah dreidel with a leather jacket and a brown mop
Singing *Come and get your love* along with Redbone
Spit your truth via reptilian microphone.
Haters say you blew it against Thanos, but that's a fallacy.
Thanos was gonna Thanos regardless, you stay
a Guardian of the Galaxy!

HULK WILL SMASH

The iconic Hulk quote peppering
our collective conscious like
a hailstorm of Hawkeye arrows
is *Don't make me angry, you wouldn't
like me when I'm angry*—

a legacy of Bill Bixby, who plays
the misnomered David Banner
in the '80s TV series, eyes
flashing green before his shirt rips
and his jeans shred and he transforms
into pre-CGI Lou Ferrigno topped
with a Jimmy Connors haircut.

In the new M.C.U., Mark Ruffalo
plays The Hulk as a smiling scientist
with glasses and an oversized doctor's
coat—*The Big Guy* Bruce can summon
to save the planet when Cap's shield
and Tony's armor prove not enough
and the only way not to succumb
is to unholster the great green gun.

These Hollywood Hulks are more digestible,
but the original grey-skinned Incredible
Hulk, who mutates emerald in Issue #2,
does not joke, does not respond to any

fateful summons, does not issue warnings
or offer irritating strangers a back-off ramp.

That Hulk gives no damn when the dam
bursts and the shirts tear and the pants shred.

He hungers only to smash.

Hulk will smash!

His giant fists factory pistons pummeling
whatever stumbles in his path—villain,
village, rhino, buffalo, building, cruise ship.

Hulk will smash!

Perhaps a primeval urge to unchain
our organic animality. Some say
he's a metaphor for nuclear holocaust.
Lord, what have we unleashed with this
prodigious beast who leaps
from city to city and pulverizes
skyscrapers, shopping malls,
hospitals, football stadia?

Hulk will smash!

Yes, in his heart, this olive-tinged
Frankenstein feels something—call
it, maybe, mercy—for Betty Ross,
but her general father knows better,
the monster's unmuzzled anger
harkens unmatched danger.

Blanket him with bullets!
Murder him with missiles!

He must be undone,
for the angrier he gets,

the stronger he becomes.

Is he an arms race?

A manifestation of male ego?

Does not his embattled roar
resemble the mouth of rage

    screaming

at Elizabeth Eckford
when she attempts
to desegregate Little
Rock Central High
School?

Yet, do we not cheer
when the green Grendel
spits out the General's
bullets and raises
his fists?

Who, after all, needs
an AR-15 when your
forearm can fracture
a space station?

Who needs a flagpole
turned spear when one
punch can topple
a pyramid?

How much
do we love
ruin?

How much
do we love
rubble?

How much
do we love
flame?

VILLAINELLE

Who is the most dastardly villain in the room?
What's more vile, vast power or a twisted sadistic brain?
Magneto, Baron Zemo, Green Goblin, or Dr. Doom?

Is evil nurtured by hurt, or does it nest in the womb?
Does Sandman by nature make lethal each grain?
Who is the most dastardly villain in the room?

Osborn cackles when Gwen Stacy plummets to her tomb
Latverians scurry beneath the steel of tyrannical reign
Magneto, Baron Zemo, Green Goblin, or Dr. Doom?

Thanos snaps the universe into a half-decade of gloom
The Kingpin's bone-crushing fist bloodies faces with pain
Who is the most dastardly villain in the room?

Galactus vacuums planet-cores, clouds whole worlds mushroom
Bullseye's pencil pierces a neck's most vulnerable vein
Magneto, Baron Zemo, Green Goblin, or Dr. Doom?

Every battle we survive, disaster yet looms
Loki snickers, betrays for personal gain
Who is the most dastardly villain in the room?
Magneto, Baron Zemo, Green Goblin, or Dr. Doom?

II.

THE THING ABOUT
THE THING

I.

In the basement of the Traceys' house,
while our parents sipped eggnog upstairs,
we played Muggison Avenue, the two
Tracey boys, the three Manelski boys,
my two brothers and me.

Rules of the game—

      none.

Procedures of the game—

turn off the lights,
swing your fists
as hard as you can.

Did anyone get hurt?

We all got hurt.

Did anyone get hurt bad?

My memory says no, but who
can really be sure? Tears flowed
every Christmas, no doubt, for that's

when we got together, parents a bit
tipsy, sons celebrating the birthday
of the Prince of Peace by slugging
each other's faces in the dark.

My signature move—

stealth

Move soft and quick like Black
Panther, hide behind a chair
and when someone slithers
past, reach out with the lightning
speed of Quicksilver, grab somebody's
shirt collar, bash them in the ear
with an elbow.

Being bashed in the ear hurts. I know.
I was bashed many times, made my own
hot tears. But I never ran upstairs to squeal.
None of us did. We took whatever elbows
and fists found us and we searched the murk
for bodies upon which we could respond
in kind.

Cloistered behind a chair, swallowing
my breath so no one could hear it, more
than anything, I wanted to be from Yancy
Street, where The Thing grew up as battling
Ben Grimm.

I didn't know where Yancy Street was,
somewhere in Brooklyn near the hospital
where I was born? Turns out it was Lower
East Side, and actually Delancey, but I never
took time to research it, just like we didn't care
about the connotations of naming our game after
Madison Avenue, thoroughfare of shiny office
buildings and slick, gimmicky advertisers.

In our fancy holiday clothes,
we traipsed down the stairs,
made the basement dark,
and swung.

II.

It is said the cosmic rays that bathed
the Fantastic Four brought out extreme
versions of each future hero.

Reed Richards morphed into Mr. Fantastic,
limbs as stretchable as his imagination

Johnny, hothead lover of hot rods
and hot women, became the Human
Torch

Susan Storm, only woman among
the quartet, had little choice
but to be Invisible

and Big Ben Grimm,
brawler born of bruising
thugs, became the monstrous

Thing with four-fingered
fists of orange rock.

In the Marvel Universe, superpowers are often
less a blessing, more a curse, but who has it worse
than Benjamin Jacob Grimm?

Johnny and Susan look smoking
in the uniforms glazing their skin.

Reed invented for himself elastic fabric
so he can reach whatever needs reaching.

The Thing gets a freakin' Speedo
as if he's a tacky tourist eating
a corn dog on the Coney Island
boardwalk.

His skin looks like dried-up mud, cracked
and fissured, as if he were dunked in a vat
of sticky pet food that adhered to his frame
like glue. The chunky ledge that substitutes
for his eyebrows could hold a flock
of a thousand pigeons. For Chrissakes

ya Yancy Street bums

the guy doesn't even merit a proper costume.
He's got a goddamned bathing suit, a frickin'
tricycle when his teammates are driving

Cadillacs

and worst of all

he can't change back.

There's no un-donning

the slick blue supersuit

for him

oh no, not for Ben Grimm

he'll never be human

he's 24-7

rough-rock skin.

III.

Marvel lore suggests Big Ben Grimm's
metamorphic mug manifests the secret thug
alter-ego of his creator Jack Kirby, Kirby
himself the not-so-secret alter ego
of his creator Jacob Kurtzburg, Kurtzburg
the creation of Rose and Benjamin, a duo
who fled Austria to escape the torches
of pogrom.

Benjamin followed a trove of Jews
into the garment industry on the Lower
East Side and Jacob grew up near Delancey
where boy-gangs fought to stake claims
and sculpt glistening American names
that wouldn't betray their membership
in the sad, scared class of people who
abandoned the shtetl in fear.

IV.

Regarding the bags of Anti-Semitic
Hate Literature left on driveways
throughout Ann Arbor on the dawn
of the Jewish New Year, this year.

To be honest, when I first walked past them
with my bad-ass runty rescue pup—a twenty-
five-pound mutt who loves to run with huskies
four times his size—I thought another dog-walker
had inadvertently dropped a bag of treats. It was
the same kind of sandwich-sized Ziploc bag
with what appeared to be a bunch of Thing-
skin-looking kibbles nestled inside.

My Spidey sense did not tingle.

When I picked up the bag, wet
with morning rain, aiming to gain
it before my dog chewed it to bits
and devoured his daily caloric intake
in a single savage blitz, I realized
what I thought were nuggets of dried dog
food were kernels of uncooked corn.
Their utility, apparently, to weigh
down the bag so its contents – a leaflet
explaining how Jews scheme with their
nefarious ways to give birth to *every single
aspect* of Covid, abortion, mass immigration,
gun control, Disney-infused pedophilia,
gay-grooming, the Biden administration,
and a global media which barks as we see fit—

wouldn't float away in the wind.

V.

As a kid, I once read '70s era
African-American slugger
for the Philadelphia Phillies,
Dick Allen, said third baseman
Mike Schmidt was the *baddest
White Boy he ever knew.*

I wanted to be the baddest Jew.

Slammed weights through twelve sets
of twelve on the basement bench press,
woke every morning with fifty push-ups
and sit-ups, wanted my shoulders
to hunker like boulders, did not, like
my Hebrew School classmates, want
to float lobs on the tennis court or finesse
somebody with a dipsy-do on the soccer pitch.

I wanted to be a bulkier Ty Cobb, a snarling
rock with sharp spikes and the dirtiest, blood-
smudgiest uniform in the park, a wrestler with
the thickest forearms and most inescapable
cross-face cradle.

Off the field or mat, I wanted to be,
dare I say it, a mild-mannered Clark
Kent, but when that umpire cried
Play ball, I wanted the fire within
to blaze. I wanted to morph
into a sonuvabitch with skin like
a mountain, a craggy hard heart
and a forehead even harder.

When the whistle blew,
it was time to clobber.

VI.

Benjamin Jacob Grimm, prodigal son of Yancy
Street, announces his Jewishness in a 1976 Hanukah
card sent by Jack Kirby to friends and family.

In the black-and-white drawing, a menorah
flares in the background, the hinge of The Thing's
mouth a whimsical Mona Lisa grin as if he couldn't
be more at peace with his day off from battling
Dr. Doom, and instead communes with a history
more mammoth even than his own. He sports
a yarmulke like a crown atop his rocky dome
and a prayer-tallis draped over his oil-drum
shoulders.

In his four-fingered fists, he holds a bible,
presumably open to the tale of Judas
Maccabee burning oil for eight days
while under siege. Judas, loosely

translated in Jew-hate, means
backstabber; Maccabee, loosely
translated from Hebrew, means
hammer, as in, when in battle

this warrior
is a *hammer.*

The God of Thunder wields
Mijölnir, but the Jew made
of rocks gets no mystical
weapon.

He must, himself,
be the hammer

use only his own
fists to clobber.

VII.

Hank Aaron, who received death threats
when he approached Babe Ruth's home
run record, was known as Hammerin'
Hank, a moniker reminiscent of Old John
Henry, the legend who pounds through rock
while racing the Industrial Revolution,
and perishes as a prize for winning.

The Golem, according to the Museum
of Judea in Berlin, is a mystical creature
formed out of earth, dirt, rock, or clay.

It is conjured, evoked, as if a John Henry–
like ghost, to rescue a Jewish community
in peril.

If I had a hammer, Pete Seeger sang

at a concert my parents took me to
when I was ten, *I'd hammer
in the morning, I'd hammer
in the evening, all over
this land. It's the hammer
of justice ...*

VIII.

Maccabee, according
to Jewish folklore, is
an acronym of the Hebrew
prayer, *Mi kamokha ba'
elim Adonai?* Who among
the gods is like you, O,
Adonai?

Who among the heroes you drew
is like you, oh, Jacob Kurtzburg?

Who among the heroes you drew
is like me?

IX.

The sentiment expressed on Kirby's
Thing card says, *Remembering you
at Hanukkah/And hoping you will find/
That your holiday leaves/ many special
memories behind.*

Benign, I suppose;
but where lies
any mention
of love?

Is love, too,

something
not for you,
Ben Grimm?

Something special—
like being human—
to leave behind?

X.

The Puppet Master crafts puppets
from radioactive clay. Sculpts them
with his hands to resemble his enemies.
In cover art for *Fantastic Four # 8*—
that looks like nothing if not nefarious-
eyebrowed scheming Jew propaganda—
the Puppet Master perches above
his puppet-people and pulls
their strings, controlling *every
single aspect* of their behavior.

He is no Jew, this manipulator of men
and minds, but he murders one. Jealous
of the wealth of Jacob, his business partner,
he blows up their lab with Jacob in it. Also
injured in the explosion is Jacob's daughter
Alicia, who loses her sight in the blaze.

With only her hands and whatever
special memories are left behind
to guide her, Alicia too becomes
a sculptor. When she touches
the rocky cheek of The Thing,
she thinks, *His face feels strong
& powerful! And yet, I can sense
a gentleness to him—there's some-
thing tragic—something sensitive!*

XI.

Change me back to Ben Grimm,
The Thing begs Reed Richards.
Find a way to let Alicia's hands
touch my human skin.

XII.

I don't remember it happening, but
the story is legend in my family. A
mythical group of motorcyclists terror-
izes our neighborhood with their roar
and my father, scrawny environmental
lawyer, emerges from the Baxter Building
of our suburban home to tell them to slow
down, *Kids like to play in this street.*

One biker, a solid block of concrete
over six feet, leather-jacketed and broad,
hits the brakes on his Harley and steps off
to shove in the chest the man who dares
scold him.

At that point, my brother, five, and I,
four, leap into the void

      plastic swords unsheathed

      and beat the blue-jeaned legs

of the invader

      urging him to leave our solar
      system alone.

      He laughs, hits
      the gas

zooms off

into space.

XIII.

At long last, Mr. Fantastic fully extends
his elastic brain, figures out how
to reverse the cosmic blast

> and rescues
> the Jew
> from his misery.

And then Ben Grimm is no
longer capable of clobbering.

He can sucker-punch here and there, but
as far as confronting evil head on, he's done,

a bystander with a pretty girlfriend who can
pet his smooth cheek.

This new tweak leaves him with the belief
Alicia will no longer love him. He's too weak.
The Fantastic Four has become a Fantastic Three.

No longer a hero

what is he?

XIV.

When my cleat caught in the unforgiving
earth and I tore the ligaments in my knee
like fishing line snapped in the jaws
of the sea, I asked myself the same
question.

If I can't run down fly balls
in centerfield, if I can't hammer
doubles into the gap

what am I?

XV.

Recipe for making a Golem:

Earth
Dirt
Clay
Jews in peril

Mix until fist.

XVI.

In 1897, an article in the *New York Times*
states, *A gang of ruffians who infest
the neighborhood of Orchard and Ludlow
Streets made a raid upon the headquarters
of the Brotherhood of Tailors. Blows
were struck, hair and whiskers were
pulled. Several men were badly injured
before the police could be informed,
and when the bluecoats were on the way,
the ruffians vanished.*

XVII.

Change me back, Ben Grimm
pleads to Reed Richards.

Make me again

a clay thing.

XVIII.

Alicia eventually falls in love
with the Silver Surfer, his glossy
gleaming skin the most perfect
opposite of The Thing's rocks.

Benjamin Jacob Grimm, alone
again, clenches his four-fingered
fists and swings.

XIX.

I like to think of myself as Muggison Avenue's
most perfect denizen. I am not afraid of the dark.
I am not afraid of being hit hard in the ear, jaw,
or eye. I am not afraid of circling someone's neck
with my forearm.

Perhaps it is the Maccabee in me. My great-
grandfather Max was a tailor. He fled
pogroms in Russia and settled in Perth
Amboy, New Jersey. Changed his name
to Kass from Kokoshky. Nobody ever
changed it back.

On Christmas, I was a young boy
burning, afraid to back down
from a fight. We turned

off the lights

and I turned

ruffian.

XX.

I have been afraid of love, it's true.
I have believed myself too ugly
to love. That's true too.

In the spring of 1981, I was also
a coward. When we played Scarsdale,
a neighboring town believed to be
inhabited by many Jews, the Junior
Varsity Baseball Coach gathered
us in a pregame circle and declared
the only other Jewish player and me
captains for the day. Then he called
the team we were about to face Scarsburgh.

I did nothing. Said nothing. Marched
along with my teammates toward
the foul line to warm up.

In the dark
on Christmas

I swung a fist
and hit Christian
kids

as well as my own
brothers. It felt good

to taste blood
in my mouth.

It felt good

to clobber.

III.

ODE TO THE MARRIAGE BETWEEN LED ZEPPELIN AND THOR

When you unleash that driving guitar,
those pounding drums, that *ahh-ah-ahhh-ah*
that sounds like a gas pedal on the last lap
of the race track, that sounds like Nolan Ryan
rearing back to throw his roaring fastball
that sounds like an avalanche about to cascade
through a valley of villains, we know

It's on!

Doesn't matter if the bad guy is a titan
from before the universe was born, doesn't
matter if he/she/it is constituted of pure dark
matter, frozen frost giant, eternal elfin evil
or every cannon that's ever been fired in every
war, Thor is about to do his God of Thunder thing
where his eyes blaze blue and his hammer swings
like a scythe, and you, Bad Guy, ain't nothing
but a sheaf of sugarcane about to be sliced, diced
and dissected—

We come from the land of the ice and snow
from the midnight sun where the hot springs flow

Oh, don't we all wish we had that kind of theme song
that wedding of drums, guitar and scream that pulls
from our ribs the Godhammer within?

47

Oh, Thor, Oh, Zeppelin, you were born to fight
as one, would that we too can find our rhythm
our own dancing, daring *ahh-ah-ahhh-ah*—our
own twanging, throbbing tango of fight and not flee
our own rumbling rhumba of release the hand
from around our necks … We are too wild
for these chains!

IF DREAMS ARE WINDOWS INTO THE LIVES OF OUR MULTIVERSAL SELVES

like Dr. Strange says, then in some universe
I am perpetually tardy to Algebra II Trigonometry,
my homework unconjured, my grade hinging
on a test for which I did not study.

In this same cyclone-swirl dreamscape
I am also late to a college baseball game,
and don't have cleats or uniform pants,
or time to return home to fetch them.
And, look, it's a game I'm actually slated
to play in, all the other backup catchers
lain low by mono. It's my big chance,
my *shot* to show off my cannon arm,
my quick bat, and now sorry, it's just
like the coaches always presumed,
I'm a talent-forsaken goon. I mean,
come on, this dang scrub can't help
but show up cleatless, pantsless, and late,
and didn't even do his math homework
in eleventh grade.

Or take this unstately morning when I woke
after dreaming a universe where I was visiting
a university attended by my high school buddy
Dan Bobker, who I haven't talked to in a quarter-
century but who now makes movies, including *Ophelia*
starring someone named Daisy Ridley, and in this alternate

destiny, she nymphily whispers to her boyfriend Hamlet,
as if she's some kind of magic elf-prophet,
nothing is as it seems, though she still winds up
drowning in the swirl of a stream, and in my dream
the college boasts a courtyard bustling with youthful
sloth and I am younger and thinner and witty and manage
to charm a woman who appears to be a cross between Daisy
Ridley and Elizabeth Olsen's Scarlet Witch, which might
sound dreamy or at least fiery, but she kissed me dryly
on the lips and it felt crusty and Dan was concurrently
consuming a burrito oozing sour cream and guacamole
and had a linguistics assignment he found confounding
and I said I'd do it gladly, it would only take me five minutes,
something to do with the sound of the letter "O" and the sound
of the letter "F" when they're kissing, *oof,* I remember thinking
while charming this woman, her hair windblown like Ophelia's
or the Scarlet Witch's, and we suck in our breaths when we make
an "O" sound, our lips forming a circle, and, when making the "F"
sound, do nearly the opposite pushing our breath outward, our lips
again circling, *oof,* this whole "O-F" process something like kissing,
and perhaps that's what I said that was so charming amidst this court-
yard of students courting, and I felt like a genius, but had
no notebook on which to inscribe my opus, we were at a college
and no one had access to any writing surface

my goodness

nevertheless

like Elizabeth Warren (not Olsen) I persisted, but switched it
to the University of Michigan where I was no longer writing
for Dan Bobker but my former student Adam Falkner
who wrote his own poetry opus called *the willies.*
I'm back in my fifties and no longer skinny but still
insisting it will only take me a quintet of minutes
to solve the linguistics and the universe has grown
paperless. I try the notes app on my iPhone,
but the screen freezes, resisting, and the elf-
prophet is hissing *keep thinking, your minutes*

are dwindling, and in this reckoning, I'm think-
ing two "Os" after an "F" can sound like *oooh*
as in fool or food but stick that "L" in between
in this dream and the sound is *uhh* as in flood,
and if this transition hisses, swishes and sucks
like a transmission floundering through mud—

Friends, please comprehend my journey through
the multiverse has no ends, only scattered
beginnings—Oh, Ophelia, we could heal ya, oh,
squealing wheel rolling between universes, let us reverse
ya, reseal ya—oh, Lord of Ruined Writing, can we
agree there's something cheap about this infinite
plot trick, this timescape of limitless rivering
where losing can always become winning,
if we just stick with it a different minute,
we can always revisit, migrate sideways, re-begin
it, rest a spell then re-spin it, if we can't lose,
why grieve, nothing's ever finished—let's just
re-spin, re-begin—*oof*—then win it.

ON OPENING DAY, I'M SORRY I'M NOT ORORO

I promised these seven and eight-year-old boys
if they practice hard, they would get better.

When you throw, hold the ball with two
fingers, not the whole hand. Use a claw
not a paw.

Step straight to the pitcher when you swing.
Attack the ball, keep the back foot in place
and let it pivot. No twirling around like
a ballerina.

They worked all winter long at an indoor
cage, heard me say over and over *practice
the fundamentals properly and you won't
learn bad habits.*

They have seen their bats smack with deeper
resonance. They have seen ground balls make
homes in their gloves. They have seen me take
checks from the hands of their parents and two
weeks later produce mystical boxes filled
with jerseys, hats, sweatshirts.

Now they see puddles on the field stretch
and river. They look at me with eyes
nearly as wet. Eyes that want to know
why I can't command the sky.

RED SKULL LIMERICK

There once was a man diabolical
Hateful in every atom and molecule
His brain schemed year after year
To make Cap disappear
But fashioned only a lack of hair follicles

ARACHNID-BITTEN, THEN SMITTEN

Peter Parker, you lucked out with what you got, son.
Ain't nobody smokin' hot like Mary Jane Watson.
Yeah, you're a nerd and a toxic spider bit you,
but when I strut through, you ain't gonna know
what hit you. You might have battled Dock Ock,
Sandman, and the Goblin, but, Tiger, it's your heart
I'm redhead robbin.' I'll be gobbling up your midnights
and your mornings. Meet me one time, leave you longing.
Look how hard it was to shed that Venom alien. I'll weave
my web inside your denim, breathe your love life back
to life like Pygmalion. Oh, yes, your genes yearn to unify
with the church of MJ. Trust me, that's what them say.
Aunt May knows that I slay, but you're clueless chronic
like Dr. Dre. Need to elevate your game like Doctor J.
You had no clue you need a new boo, brain gunked
with spider glue, hole in your head where the Vulture
flew, lost in Mysterio's misty brew, you missed
your chance 'til issue # 42. Time to whittle down
your crew to just me and you. You thought you knew
your aunt was faking like a chatbot, but when you
opened up that door, *Face it, Tiger, you just hit
the jackpot!*

BLACK BOLT

I am the big bad wolf who cannot blow.
If I open my mouth, I can shake a city
to dust. If I keep my mouth open, I
can obliterate a planet. Maybe
you think that's tragic, like I'm
a larger, more violent Little Mermaid,
my voice locked forever behind my teeth.

But you won't see me blabbering
my insecurities like Spider-Man
or Hawkeye. You won't see me
cranking my square jaw to offer
self-righteous blather like Captain
America.

Ever been stuck in a conversation
where you were expected to say
something, maybe in a staff
meeting, or during Trivia Night
at the bar, where you feel that
pressure like a fish hook pulling
at your lips to chime in with
an opinion about something
you don't care about?

I haven't.

Ever sit at a table at a wedding
reception and feel obligated
to talk to the guest next to you?
To engage in that dull as a dead
radiator dance—*Do you know
the bride or the groom?*

Not me.

Ever say something awkward
that makes you feel like a hot
spotlight found your embarrassed
forehead and you're transported back
to the all-alone middle of a middle
school cafeteria with the whole
building's monstrous population
consuming you with oozing eyes?

Ever open your mouth wide
when you have something
really important to say
and that whooshing sound
you hear is the flock
of bats screaming into
your cavernous, empty
throat when no one gives
a single damn about
the vibration of your
vocal cords?

When I speak

the whole world

shudders

TRUE BELIEVER

I was one

who read
the letters
to the editor
at the backs
of comic books.

Perhaps I simply
wanted to savor
more pages, didn't
want the too skimpy
narrative to finish.

If it did, after
all, what was
next?

A trip to the back-
yard to rake leaves?

A pile of problems
flipping fractions

or swimming
through the vis-
cous murk of long

division?

Did I believe
everything I
read?

Truly, I did not.

I did not think

a witch clad
in scarlet would
ever marry a metal
machine. Nor did I
believe Wolverine
would ever have
a sabertoothed killer
for a brother.

Still, when Stan Lee
deemed me True
Believer

it meant I was part
of a community my
parents and teachers
did not understand.

I did not need to be
reading *The Red Badge
of Courage* or *The Yearling*.
I did not need to be reading
Johnny Tremain or that
book about ferns.

I was part of a tribe who
knew the difference between
the two Human Torches;
who understood the Lizard

was no grotesque hybrid reptile
worthy of being reviled, but only
a scientist sadly misguided.

Listen, when I grunted
through twelve sets
of twelve on the bench
in my parents' basement

I wanted my triceps
to burn and harden.

There would come a moment,
I was sure of it, when, during
a field trip, a bridge would
collapse, or perhaps, a wall
of our school would crumble
due to shelling from the Soviet
Union

and the girl I had a crush
on would be pinned beneath
a block of cement, her demise
imminent, and I would show up
just in time, flex
my new muscles,
lift the deadly debris

and save her.

Was it foolish, Mr. Lee,
for me to believe myself
a savior?

Truly, it was.

I have grown to accept
I will never prevent
the demolition of a bridge

using solely the brick
of my chest. But also—

once on the highway,
when I was maybe thirteen
and my father was driving,
we passed an overturned
station wagon, the driver's
panicked face trapped upside
down behind the steering wheel.

Though we were on our way
to a family vacation and time
was already crunching—we
were on the cusp of missing
our ferry—

my father
did not
hesitate.

"We have to stop," he told us.
"We have no choice."

Was it foolish, Mr. Lee, for me
to believe I was strong enough
to help if needed, that if it came
to unwedging that woman from
the driver's seat, I could be part
of a human Jaws of Life?

Truly, it was not.

I kept lifting weights
long after that middle-
school crush exhausted
its fuel. I believe a man
without fear is a man
who already knows

what fear feels like
and is willing to feel
it again. I believe
anger can sometimes
make me stronger.
I believe the difference
between Captain America
and the Red Skull runs
deeper than geography.

I believe there is right.

There is just.

And there is true.

Truly, I believe that.

 I do.

IV.

JUNGLE ACTION #6 - #17

SEPT. 1973 - SEPT. 1975,

"PANTHER'S RAGE"

I was left behind with the immensity of the existing things.
A sponge, suffering because it cannot saturate itself

—Csezlaw Milosz

I.

Can you come home again, Black Panther?

In the Valley of Serpents, fetid heat
choking your breath, you are lashed
to a cactus. Every time you move, spikes
lacerate your already oozing wounds.

You were left to die by Salamander
K'Ruel, minion of Killmonger,
wannabe ruler with a penchant
for murdering innocent villagers.

Can you come home to Wakanda,
T'Challa, after your two-year sabbatical
fighting beside Earth's Mightiest Heroes?

Control your breathing, you shout
inside your head, *shut out the pain.* You think
of your father T'Chaka, who told you on a sun-
drenched afternoon when you were ten, *You must*

master the arts of manhood —but if you learn
them at the expense of the art of childhood,
my son, you will learn only self-deception.

A lizard crawls across your tattered body, licks
your blood, ceases to sip from your eyes
only when a rush of air startles it, a pterodactyl's
flapping wings as it dives to devour its prey.
You are finished, T'Challa, leaking flesh crucified
on a cactus, but, lucky you, the great monster's talons
lash your bindings instead of your chest.

Is it any surprise, Panther, when you
arm-lock the neck of the Pterodactyl,
swing upward as if you are flipping
through a grade school playground
and ride the beast through the sky
like a horse?

II.

Can you come home to Wakanda, T'Challa?

When you torque a palm tree
into a catapult, launch a boulder
into the forehead of a Tyrannosaurus

When you impale the giant alabaster
gorilla on the bones of his ancestors
after he endeavors to throw you off
the rim of a glacier

When you escape the mind muck
of King Cadaver in his horrific hall
of mirrors

When your most trusted advisors
believe you've been corrupted

by outworlders

When half your warriors
switch allegiance
to Killmonger

When your lover is framed
for a palace court murder

When you smash the skull
of Baron Macabre who strangled
young Kantu's father

When you battle Venomm's pythons
and the vibranium spear-tip of Malice

When you wrestle Lord Karnaj
and Sombre, each of whom flash
within a whisker of your slaughter

as if you must complete twelve
Herculean tasks to regain the faith

of your people

do you lose track
of the sunset, T'Challa,

do you lose track
of the dawn?

III.

The poet Taku tells Venomm
in the royal prison, *Our fears
and desires should not be
scorned*

Venomm, chuckling
snake charmer,

disagrees

—the world's had educated
guys leading ... shootin'
off their big mouths
for what?

Flowery speeches
to please each other
is all it comes down to

T'Challa, when you left Wakanda
to fight with the Avengers, was it
the promise of fame that lured
you?

Was it acceptance in the land
of American flag, American
White, American steel?

When you take an American lover,
is it any wonder Killmonger unlocks
a door to owning your kingdom?

Panther, is it possible to drink
the immensity of two worlds?

IV.

When Sombre sinks to his muddy grave,
a sprite, crouched in a tree in the land
of your father, asks, *Does this man's*
death mean you have won, Intruder?

Are you an intruder

in your own country,
Black Panther?

Revolutions give one the illusion
they are doing something with
their lives, Taku tells Venomm.

You ain't always right, Taku,
Venomm says. *Revolutions*
change things and sometimes
those changes are better'n
what's gone before.

V.

You clamber to the top
of Warrior Falls
for the final battle.

Killmonger! you shout,
This is where it ends!

Killmonger swings
his spiked belt
through your ribs,
soaking your skin
with blood.

When you fall, you won't
be getting up again, T'Challa,
the revolutionary thunders

just a corpse in a torn uniform
whose meaning will soon
be forgotten.

Can you come home
to Wakanda, T'Challa?

Run, Kantu, run full out,
the nine-year-old boy
screams inside his head,

run past the cemetery
where your father, killed
by Killmonger's Macabre,
lies separated from you
forever by volcanic earth.

Run, Kantu! There is
no time for mourning...

Panther, you proclaim,
I am no longer a slave
to the shadows of doubt,
your fists battering
Killmonger's face.

You've wanted the same thing I have
all along, haven't you, Killmonger
answers with laughter and lifts you

above his head the way a child might
lift a rock to smash it against the concrete
of a preschool parking lot—*This time,*

Killmonger boasts

I'll break your back-
bone and stand over
you

Run, Kantu, run!

Run to the Falls, scream
your rage as Killmonger
screams his

as The Panther
screams his

Run, Kantu, run!

With all your nine-year-old strength
hurl your shoulder into the heart
of the man standing on the cliff-edge

who murdered your father

widowed your mother

Run, Kantu, run!

*It is over with a silent descent. Kill-
monger hits the crashing white rapids
and disappears under the surface.*

*Neither the Panther
nor Kantu speak.*

Can you come home
to Wakanda, T'Challa?

*They walk into
the familiar sun*

The rage of Warrior
Falls thunders against
rock.

Can you
come home
again, T'Challa?

What is your rite

of return?

In the frothing

rapids, the blood

of revolution

churns.

V.

IN PRAISE OF THE PYM PARTICLE

Imagine…

      being able

to shrink   or grow

like, oh, Jeff, oh
no, where'd he go?

Hey, yo, it's rich, you feel that itch?
I'm chilling twixt your eyebrows.

What, how? Oh, wow, crawling now
'cross your clavicle. Dang, this Pym
Particle's radical.

No? You think you can slap
me like a bug, be defiant?
I flip the script, I'm towering
giant. My massive dome busts
your house-roof, you're terrified
now, you timid mouse, oops, I'm even
bigger now you mini-louse, whoot!

Call the choppers in but they can't shoot me
sorry, I shrank again. Dancing on the tip
of your epi-pen, I'm guzzling Pympenephrine
the quantum realm

hella zen

mediating

levitating

past Shaq

the Pym Daddy Mack

dunks on every rim. Thanks to you,
Hank Pym, I own the gym, people
in the bleachers tweaking like *Oh,
who's him?* He's that dude in the Ant
Man suit. Try to smoosh him with
your boot, oh shoot, scoot, scoot
now he's under the tree root, your
brain falling out your head, need
a parachute. The point is moot
he's growing massive brute
the huge galoot, too astute
angles all acute, sharper
than a kitchen knife, a wind-
mill scythe, never know
where I'm gonna be or what
height. I own the lows *and* highs
now you salty like McDonald's
fries. Forget Bill Nye. Who's the Supa
Fly Science Guy? Can't be spotted
by the human eye, so sly, mini-spy
oh my * sigh *

now Goliath
in the sky.

IRON MAN GHAZAL

What matters is keeping the heart ticking under armor
Few of us can be gods, wielding thunder armor

It's tempting to believe we'll die if we do not—when battles
are dire—conjure and wire complex wonder armor

Sometimes we battle evils too vile and their weapons
pierce our mettle, slash and cleave asunder armor

We stumble and crumble, our repulsor rays fail
and we Icarus-fall, weighed down by our blunder armor

It is then our hearts dwindle to their last stark spark
we nearly flame off, our torch sputters burnt umber armor

Yet, we must not give up, must reconnect our blood
to the tick. We are lost in unfeeling, number armor

We are all rusted men some days, all clink, clank and clunk.
You too, Jeff, sometimes stink, stank, and stunk, don some

humbler armor.

MARVEL COMICS CONVENTION

MADISON SQUARE GARDEN, 1976

"I can't believe I took four ten-year-old boys
by myself on a train to Manhattan," my mother
says, decades later. My personal mission—

requisition an original *Daredevil #47, "Brother,
Take my Hand,"* the iconic issue where DD
befriends Willie Lincoln, a soldier blinded

by shrapnel in Vietnam. Lincoln ends up
mixed up with gangsters back in Hell's
Kitchen and Daredevil pummels some

on a stairwell, a melee memorialized on the issue's
cover where the Man Without Fear swings upside-
down, one hand on the banister, his red boots

smacking one thug in the face while another, already
smacked, tumbles backward toward a third. In a life-
threatening moment, Daredevil stretches his crimson

gauntlet toward Lincoln to save him from falling
and DD in his unmasked identity as Matt Murdock
extends a symbolic hand in how to believe

in oneself when the world appears always
in darkness. The brotherhood between
the three—Murdock, Lincoln, and DD—

is a brotherhood of feeling with fingers to find
a way forward, but also a brotherhood that reaches
across race. To fifth-grade me it meant I too

could find brothers beyond borders and we could
support each other on the ballfield, in the wrestling
room, in the cafeteria when flirting. Originally

published in December, 1968, the issue sold
for 12 cents, but 8 years later, when we trooped
crosstown with my mother from Grand Central

Station to Madison Square Garden, I knew it
would cost at least 5 bucks out of the 15 I had
with me, birthday money I clutched tightly

inside my front pocket when we trafficked
into the sacred edifice where Earl the Pearl
hooped and scooped and Clyde Frazier

fluttered and buttered. The floor buzzed
like a giant wasp, loud and chaotic, a thousand
glistening tables and ten times that many people.

My mother struggled with surveillance as we
fantastic four wide-eyes scattered and dug
for comics like Moloids. It wasn't long before

I rescued DD 47, in pretty good condition
swathed in plastic for $6.67. Most new
issues were selling for a quarter so I could

likely snag a couple more vintage mags
and still fill my bag with an abundance
of Cap, Rawhide Kid, and Black Panther

to read on the train back to the suburbs. Heck,
I might even sequester a buck I could splurge
on a lemon-flavored Italian ice at the refreshments

booth. In truth, the adventure seemed
a phenomenal success until I noticed
the distress of one of my buddies

when he fished into his pocket for his money
and found a cosmic void worthy of a Captain
Marvel voyage. Was his fistful of dough stolen

forgotten in the train's seat cushions, or had
he dropped it somewhere along the Avenue
of the Americas? Nobody, not even one

of the nearby adult dudes dressed
as a S.H.I.E.L.D. agent, could answer
that question and while the rest

of us stuffed our bags with hero stories,
my friend's tears flowed freely having
traveled all this way to New York City

for a once-in-a-grade-school experience and now
with no power in his pocket, he, like Peter Parker
when J. Jonah Jameson rejected his photos

would return
home empty.

But then as if she'd heard
the bellowing of a great bugle
and not unlike the arrival

of no-longer-dusted
heroes retrieved
from limbo

to square up against Thanos, except without
any celestial assistance, my mother, with no cape,
mask, or radar sense, reached her hand toward

my friend, whom she hardly knew, grasped
his fingers and slipped him a twenty as if he'd
shared her womb with me, and he filled his bag

with stories of Spidey, Hulk, and the Banshee
and we trooped back across the city, not holding
hands, but still clinging close so my mother could

watch over us
as if we were

brothers.

NICK FURY LIMERICK

There once was a commando who howled
Battled Nazis with Cap, face uncowled
Became a superspy with one eye
Chomps cigars but won't die
A hundred years old, yet unjowled

SPIDER-MANS OR
SPIDER-MEN

The question occurs to me on the way home
from *No Way Home.* The next day I pose
it to my students in English Ten—I get it
there are three of them, but are they Spider-
Mans or Spider-Men?

The answer devolves into debate
with the ultimate verdict declaring
Andrew Garfield the cutest Spidey
and I say that's surprising, you're voting
blindly, look at the wonderment of Toby
McGuire, his perpetual befuddlement,
but we've spun off on a digression
let us return to the original question.

When the trinity of web-slingers stands
against the Green Goblin, Electro,
and Sandman, is the troika of villains
confronting three distinct Spider-Mans,
or a trio of Spider-Men?

Well, says a student wearing a hoodie featuring
an airbrushed Shaquille O'Neal as a member
of the Orlando Magic, imagine Spider-Man
is not a youngish adult but a first-grader, a kid
with web-shooters who can crawl up windows
and walk across ceilings, we'd call him Spider-

Child, right? And if you had another in the same
classroom, you'd have two Spider-Childs. No
righteous teacher would ever decree they have
Spider-Children.

My students universally believe this notion
is creepy, and, indeed, I find my brain slinking
into Stephen King's *Children of the Corn,*
where nobody refers to each individual
creep-kid as a singular corn-urchin. In fact,
it's the plurality of the progeny that renders
the kids terrifying, the way they transmute
a chanting group-think of murder, pied-pipered
by He Who Walks Behind the Rows, the movie
itself a secondary crop grown out of Shirley Jackson's
The Lottery, a story echoing the long history of humanity—
when the harvest fails, or the rains won't come—how we
offer in bargain the blood of one of our own.

Whoa, I know we just got deep here, spinning an exploration
of grammar into one of human sacrifice, but such is the nature
of tenth-grade English where *Lord of the Flies* has long portended
more menace than a simple cadre of boy-kids swimming in tidepools
and constructing thatch-huts. Uncle Ben's message to Peter Parker
is *with great power comes great responsibility,* a lesson Spidey
wrestles perpetually, knowing he let the thief of the wrestling
bout's proceeds run freely—not his function to step in and stop
him—a thought process utterly debunked when the robber murders
his uncle. In that sense, Uncle Ben is the sacrifice we all must
accept for Spider-Man to protect our city from the plotting
of multiversal versions of He Who Walks Behind the Rows,
who as the Rolling Stones remind us, goes by many names
and guises, including translated from Hebrew, *The Lord
of the Flies*—who, after all, must be none other than
the Spider—for who else holdeth dominion over mortal
existence when he hisseth, *Come into my parlor?*

Is it too much spin then
to say we are all Spider-Men?

That the question is not one of grammar, but numeracy,
it's maybe our oldest story, think now of Aunt May
in the movie, or first-graders in Rwanda, Gaza, Kibbutz
Be'eri, Ukraine or Uvalde—

whose deaths are we willing
to accept, and how many?

VILLAINELLA

What the Hela? Daughter of Loki, slayer of mortals and gods.
Why destroy every scintilla of the villa where you were born?
Is your death-touch a curse, or do you consider it fortunate odds?

You sling arrows of disdain at we earth-trodding sods.
What joy you must feel, our bloody demise a few seconds of porn.
What the Hela? Daughter of Loki, slayer of mortals and gods?

Astride your killer hound, you prey, destroy our safety façade.
We mere pigs-in-a-blanket at your savage shindig, our dignity shorn.
Is your death-touch a curse, or do you consider it fortunate odds?

We cower, no match for your power, helpless peas in our pods.
You kill us and cackle, your glee a betrayal, our covenant torn.
What the Hela? Daughter of Loki, slayer of mortals and gods?

You want only subservient beadles, purveyors of nods.
A planet-wide funeral the mark of your merciless scorn.
Is your death-touch a curse, or do you consider it fortunate odds?

Stylish murderess, Hela, our bodies in bags by Coachella, we clods
of mud 'neath your heel, you heartless goddess minus office to mourn.
What the Hela? Daughter of Loki, slayer of mortals and gods,
Is your death-touch a curse, or do you consider it fortunate odds?

JUGGERNAUT

I cannot be stopped. Thor
cannot stop me with his
magic hammer. The Thing
cannot stop me with his stony
fist.

I do not cease and desist.

I just keep coming.

I bash my head against the wall
until the wall falls. I bash my head
against a warehouse until the ware-
house falls. I bash my head against
a mountain until the whole mother-
loving mass of rock quakes, trembles,
quivers, and falls.

People say the definition of insanity
is doing the same thing over and over
even when it doesn't work, like bashing
your head against a wall. But what
if bashing your head against a wall
does work?

Welcome to my world, buckos,
where my skull is harder than

any substance known to human-
kind. Where my head bashes
and bashes and keeps bashing
until whatever purports to stand
in front of me can stand
no longer.

I don't get tired. I don't feel
pain. I don't feel joy, comfort,
peace, or relief. I just bash.

What kind of life is that?

Everybody wants me when
they need something broken.

I am a hammer with the sole
mission of demolition, an unchained
bull snorting and stomping through
the China shop of the world.

I am Cain Marko.

What a stupid name.

The Mark of Cain.

The truth is my first,
last, and middle names
are all the same—

Momentum.

Remember the kid in pre-
school who knocked every-
thing beautiful to the ground,
who made other kids cry
when they built some shaky
masterpiece with blocks

and the bighead bully thundered
along and demolished it?

I am that bully.

I'm the one who stomped
through your sandcastle,
toppled your Jenga tower,
marauded through your make-
shift village of sticks and leaves.

I ruined it all.

Welcome to my world, buckos.

I'm not a force for good,
or evil, I'm just a force.

Call me when you need
something to fall down.

FRIDAY AFTERNOONS

For Brad, Doug, Mike, Joe, and occasionally Marty

After classes for the week were complete, we'd inspect
our mostly empty wallets, pool together twenty bucks,
and troop six blocks to the comic books store whose
name, sadly, I can no longer remember. There, we'd
purchase copies of the newest *Avengers, Daredevil,*
Thor, Fantastic Four, Hulk, Spider-Man, Power Man
& Iron Fist, Punisher, Captain America, X-Men,
Iron Man, Captain Marvel, or *The Defenders.*

Like third-graders, we'd spread on the floor
in the room shared by Brad and Joe and take
turns reading each new issue. Most comics
we cruised through in seven or eight minutes,
passing them from hand to hand until each
of us had deciphered them all, the whole process
Quicksilvering too quickly, lasting only maybe
an hour and a quarter.

What were we trying to escape, juniors
in college, sequestered on the top floor
of the McClellan dorm?

The world had not yet heard of Columbine or September
11th, or climate change, or Covid, yet while classmates
danced drunkenly in boxers on couches, their junk protruding

like lances, table-tent fliers in the dining hall informed
us three out of four women would be sexually assaulted
in their lifetimes, and campus-wide outcry ensued
when some dudes on the baseball team stalked through
the quad behind a gay couple and spit slurs and tapped
their bats menacingly on the sidewalk.

They were grinders—Brad and Joe and Doug
and Mike and sometimes Marty, Econ and Math
majors who worked harder than I did, my head ostriched
in Victorian novels. Amidst the turmoil, we retreated
to our hovel. Only some of us attended a Take Back
the Night march, holding candles in Dixie cups to keep
the wax from burning our hands. Did any of us speak
up to demand our teammates abandon their harassment?

Memory's blurry, but I suspect calling out teammates
unlikely. Was it enough that none of us hauled
our own bats into the night to threaten? That we
did not disbelieve the table-tent lessons?

What I mean to say is, caught
in a swirl of campus distress,
blue book tests and problem sets,
we felt winds surge through our chests
and whether or not we understood
their breath, we sought a refuge
to think and digest.

Our failure to stand stronger was, it's true,
shamefully complicit, but what we needed
in that moment, more than anything, was
to be physically present, close enough
to touch each other on dying afternoons
when the unpredictable chaos of weekend
nights beckoned.

On the fourth floor of McClellan Hall,
early evening light softening the windows,

we were boys again, nervous but hoping,
funneling through inked and colored pages
our struggles to become good men.

VI.

THE HOUR OF THANOS

For Ben Cohen
After Ross Gay, Franny Choi, and Danez Smith

De Profundis
De Profundis

Tick tock says
the Doomsday

Clock

glaciers recede in shock
terrorists flock like deadly
hawks with paraglider

claws

child-murder on both
sides of the border

De Profundis
De Profundis

bombs drop, don't stop
more children shot

at a bowling alley
in Maine
in Ukraine, bombs
drop, don't stop
more children shot

in Texas, cut taxes
and children with
razor wire strung
through the river

and the bullets
don't stop

buy an AK
in the shop
down the block

tick tock says
the cop with
knee on neck

tick tock says
the mob scaling
the Capitol façade

tick tock

pull the trigger
on the Glock

tick tock

a two-hundred pound
python slithers through
the swamp

tick tock

the email says students
must stop, antisocial
behavior

will not be
tolerated

in this spot

The Speaker
of the House
will not tolerate

people being gay

or a woman having any say
over how her body sways

De Profundis
De Profundis

The Hour of Thanos approaches

Captain America unconscious, his cowl
torn, brain concussed; Vision's skull
shattered; Bruce Banner crunched;
Scarlet Witch burned to a crisp;
Black Panther, Black Widow
Spidey, Tony Stark, all eclipsed
the world engulfed
in dark

Thor's
Stormbreaker
flung afar

The Hour
of Thanos
is upon us

hospitals in ruins
emergency rooms buried
in rubble, misinformation
spins inside the bubble

ten thousand sparrows
smash into skyscraper
windows and meet
their ends

do you send

do you send

Ruth Bader Ginsburg dead
John Lewis dead
Elon Musk brand name X

do you send

De Profundis

who is that
in the hostage
video

who is that
with the severed
limb

who is that
left alone
to fend
in the lion's
den

do you send

bombs again

what inside this skin
can resist the knife
from plunging in

bombs
again

do you send

De Profundis
De Profundis

hurricanes gather
wildfires blaze
mudslides raze
entire villages,
cities

rivers overflow
their poisonous banks
tsunamis swallow
nations with landmines
and tanks

reservoirs
saturate with
chemical rot

tick tock

another child shot
another murderous
traffic stop

tick tock

No, Thanos

No, I will not

How can I raise
this fist?

I am just
one man

What inside
my chest

can resist
this mess?

De Profund—

No, Thanos
I say thee—

In the morning
when I rise

Thanos, I do not
give a—

Bring a tear
of joy to my eyes

Thanos, I am
unhammered

and tell me
everything…

Thanos, I have
only my two arms
this heart
these shoulders

What the fuck is wrong
with you anyway, you

megalomaniacal, gro-
tesque purple infant?

Somebody use a tomato-slicer
to carve those grooves
in your chin, you goofy
opp, Grape Ape looking,
festering bruise?

Listen, you big fucking goon

I am just one person

and you are infinite

bullshit

but as long
as I own
this voice

as long as this
ordinary mouth
can utter

my God is
a vengeful God
and He has drowned
the world in flood

and He has soaked
the sea in blood

and He has toppled
the tower when our
mouths spoke the same
tongue

but, in the beginning was

the word, the fluttering
of this throat and my God

gave me this voice
this drum, my fist
is an arrow
my marrow
resolute

Thanos, I hope you got
good health insurance

'cuz you best
back the fuck up

my voice redounds
off the knaves
of a church

my voice erupts
like magma
spitting

from the bowels
of this earth

and I will sing
against these bombs

and I will sing
against these floods

and I will sing
against these fires

and I will sing
against these mobs

and I will sing
against this darkness

I will sing against
this darkness

and I don't know
if I can knock
your buster ass flat

but know this
you oversized
undersexed
sociopathic
scourge

win or lose

I am going
down

singing

VII.

ELEGY FOR BLACK WIDOW

It is said the black widow spider
is a sexual cannibal—mates, then
in order to protect her children,
devours her partner.

Natasha Romanova loved—among
others—Daredevil, Hawkeye, Hercules
Bucky Barnes, and Bruce Banner.

All wounded, all at one point
devoured to the level of teeth
chewing through bone

but not by she

of the Red Room

she trained to kill

she spun to sleek,
slink and slither

so unlike the befuddled Spider
web-slinging off the Empire State
Building, illuminated by the shine
of Broadway—the Black Widow
lives in shadow, the penumbra

of her victims stabbed through heart,
garroted around throat, shot in perfect
circle through skull

darkening always her mien.

Oh, Natasha, becoming an Avenger
is not enough redemption, is it?

Oh, Widow

we knew all along
it would be you

didn't we?

From the moment you told Bruce how
they sterilized you in the Red Room

oh, Widow

you who broke
your own face
to break free

when you informed Banner
in his towel as he emerged
from the shower

the two of you missing your moment
while downstairs in the kitchen Clint
Barton massaged the stomach
of his pregnant wife, even then

you knew

didn't you, Natasha?

A soul for a soul, the guardian of the Infinity Stone

demanded, and you told Clint you'd worked for five
years to reach this abyss. He slammed you on
the ground. You shocked him with your venom.
He shot you with an arrow and sprinted for the edge
but you leapt, ensnared him in your web, anchored
him to the ledge, you two assassins, owners of too
many sins, battling to see who would perish. You
begged him to let you go, kicked off the cliffside
when he said no, and you, Widow, fell so he might
live, so his wife and kids might un-dust and live,
so the shadow of the Red Room might, at last
dissipate to mist.

Tony got the big send-off
but it is you, Black Widow,
who, when you had the chance
to cannibalize your former lover,
chose instead to devour
yourself.

LUKE CAGE LIMERICK

There once was a hero for hire
Whose partner swung fists made of fire
Created in the shadow of *Shaft*
He fought gangsters and graft
With a tow-chain to belt his attire

DEAR BULLSEYE,

If you could dot the outside corner
with a spinning slider at the knees
every time you wanted to

If you could make Mike Trout
look like a six-year-old stepping
to the plate with a swimming noodle

If you could send Aaron Judge
hangdog back to the bench as if
you'd delivered him there via
Amazon Prime

Why would you, instead, sidearm
a playing card so it slices somebody's
throat, or hurl a ballpoint pen through
some poor sap's heart?

Look, I understand the thrill
of throwing outside the lines.
Once, in college, on the way

out of the recreation lounge
I snared a stale half-bagel
someone abandoned on the edge
of a pool table and swore I could
wing it forty feet across the room

nail the switch on the opposite wall,
and turn off the lights.

Ha ha, my roommate laughed, *no way.*
But I knew I could do it, felt the thunder
in my collarbone, bet my buddy twenty
bucks and let that bagel fly. Threw it sub-
marine-style, as if I were skipping a rock.
It cut the air like Cap's shield on an arc
from right to left, honed in like a heat-
seeking missile on the tiny switch
and *click,* the room mushroomed black.

What a thrill to master
the currents of the air!

To send a harmless object
on a precision flight path
and turn it lethal. I get it,
Bullseye. I don't know if
I've ever felt more powerful.

But to use that skill to kill?

You own no Daredevil radar-sense,
absorbed no Super-Soldier Serum,
consumed no heart-shaped herb.

Your deadly aim stems only
from obsessive practice. Thousands
of hours flinging knives, darts,
spears, silver dollars, whatever
your fingers could grasp,
until you never missed
your target.

What is so broken inside
that what you yearn to pierce
is skin?

It is you, Bullseye, I am most dis-
appointed in, whom I most abhor.
Your skill the most beautiful,
the only one I could ever claim
a sliver of attaining. If I could
have dedicated my life to practicing
the way you did, trained my technique,
my breath, my nerves, could my aim
have become as lethal as yours?

What then would I have done?

Would striking out big-league
hitters feel like enough?

Would I have been satisfied
without spilling blood?

I like to think so, but, too,
what would have been
my responsibility
to humanity?

Yes, I could have made millions playing
baseball, but what if I could have bought
into an exclusive poker game at the Kremlin
prior to Putin's invasion of Ukraine?

Would I have owed it to the world
to wing a jack of spades through
the dictator's jugular?

How many lives
could I have saved?

Bullseye, you quit a kids'
game to become an assassin.

That seems a horror,
but what's the difference
between you and our
country's finest sniper?

How much of your villainy
depends on your target?

OSBORNS

I.

Why does Osborn hair—not Willem
Dafoe's flow in the movies, but how
it's drawn in the comics—look like
chainmail?

Perhaps the tight curls twirling close
to the scalp reflect the rage coiled
beneath Norman's skin.

The Goblin lives within him.

Father figure to Peter Parker,
he too is inhabited by venom,
an envy that owns him, insisting—
in Abrahamic tradition—his pseudo-
son, high on a bridge, must choose
whom to sacrifice—a bus filled
with strangers, or his first love
Gwen Stacy?

What'll it be, Peter?

Save the bus stuffed
with people you've
never met, or rescue

your blonde-haired
sweet-hearted lover?

Possessor of great power, Parker tries
to thread the eyelet of an angel, make
the bus the priority, land it safely, and still
rescue the plunging Stacy, his self-invented
web-shooter sending a lifeline to catch her
a split-second before she smashes against
pavement.

For a moment, it appears good will triumph,
but that fairytale must exist elsewhere. Despite
the life-saving web, Gwen Stacy is already dead,
killed by her fall through the air. It's not fair.
Spidey has done all he can yet can't conquer
the Goblin, an obsession that drives him
with his own hands to want to kill him.

Is he too then fallen?

The question Miltonian—

Ultimately, is it Spidey who murders
Norman, or his own glider that impales
him?

If Spidey deals the death blow,
has the venom of vengeance
consumed him, or is the carnage
just retribution?

II.

Harry is jealous of Peter the genius. Peter
the love object of Gwen, of MJ, of Flash
Thompson. Who loves Harry Osborn?

Does even Norman?

The Goblin grows
green with envy.

The Glider has a mind
of its own making. It
conjures its own plans
for impaling.

The Goblin on the Glider
is a skywriter, a Wicked
Witch trailing smoke
from his broomstick.

Who among us can face down
our inner hiss? The cackle
that whispers unfairness?

Who among us can skywrite
as free as the sky, our exhaust
spewing only forgiveness?

III.

The Goblin never dies.

Even the Glider's impalement
cannot bury him. The Goblin
returns as a new Norman, or
a Harry-son, or a Gwen Stacy
downloaded from an alien.

The Goblin

does not always appear
as a goblin. The Glider
does not always appear

as a glider. Look, we are

flying around
in circles here.

The Goblin can become
a respected businessman.

There is precedent
for the Goblin to become
president.

Harry is to Norman
as sins are to the father
as envy is to bone.

Look, we are flying around
on witch-brooms here, every
bridge we construct encases

somebody's body
in its foundation.

Who among us can
glide, fueled only
by forgiveness?

WHEN I HAVE TO RING A KID UP
WHILE HIS FATHER YELLS AT HIM
FROM BEHIND THE BACKSTOP

I've never understood why anyone
would want to rule the world.

I'm talking to you, Ulysses Klaue,
Dr. Doom, Kingpin, assorted
other egomaniacal assholes.

Why would you want
to be in charge
of so much?

I mean, I have a hard time umpiring.

Think of a twelve-year-old kid who's
got a modicum of talent, will probably
be a decent high school player in a few
years, a pleasant enough swing, some
speed on the bases and an arm
with a moderate amount of zip.

He steps to the plate with a small hop,
looking mildly excited, generally confident,
but his dad's got a voice like a whining
power tool and he's a fortress situated
in a foldout chair, big and broad behind
the backstop as if he wants to call balls
and strikes himself.

He yells, *Get that front foot down, 22, load*
up, be aggressive, get that front foot down,
power the hips, and let's be honest, I wouldn't
call the man a galactic plague, but he sure
sounds like Banshee, who, technically, is no
bad guy, just a mutant who's briefly an X-Man
and can sharpen soundwaves until they hurt,
but this kid in the batter's box, drowning
in the barrage of his father's voice, freezes
as if Ice Man captured him in a cryogenic cage
when a very hittable fastball drifts over the middle
of the plate. Strike one. And now Dad's louder,
That's your pitch, 22, don't let that go by, be
aggressive, get *that front foot down, load up,*
get that foot down, be aggressive

and the pitcher's no dummy, he knows
this hitter's about to leap out of his socks,
swing with all his hundred-and-eleven-
pound power at whatever the next pitch
is, no matter *where* the next pitch is,
and he throws a curve that doesn't
curve much, I mean, face it, these
kids are twelve, but it's nonetheless
enough and the kid swings out of his
skin and misses the ball by a foot
when it bounces in the dirt

strike two.

Now Pops is pissed—*What are*
you swinging at, 22? You gotta be
kidding me, read that spin, 22, get that
front foot down early so you can stay
balanced, don't help the pitcher
out, 22, be patient, but stay
aggressive, guard the plate,
but get a good pitch, and now
the hitter's confidence, that little

hop into the box, has evaporated
like sweat into the cloudless sky
and the sun's heat fries him
like a potato

and here's what

I mean, Loki, now it's all on me,
dang kid shaking like a martini,
and I'm behind the plate, just
trying to do the job for which
I'm being paid 45 bucks, with
this kid's father behind me
bellowing.

Doctor of Doomness, Physician
of Fatality, do you understand
what I'm saying?

It's *my* responsibility, *all* mine,
when that next pitch sails over
the inside corner, and the trembling
kid's bat doesn't budge
from his shoulder
and *I* have to be
the villain who
declares strike three.

I have to live with knowing
he's going to hear about it
from his father for forty
minutes during the car
ride home.

I have to live with this kid maybe leaving
the game forever, or perhaps, worse, sticking
with it so his dad doesn't brand him a quitter,
but never again hopping into the box
with confidence, or joy

and that's just one twelve-year-old
in the middle of a nothing tournament
in the middle of a lengthy summer
in the middle of Michigan, and you're
talking about wanting to rule
the world?

MOLEMAN GHAZAL

Light slashes my eyes above the warm ground.
I glower and glow below rotting farm ground.

You build your monuments to war where the sun heats
bright, forget the chaos beneath, the armed ground.

You brand we who live in the dark vermin.
Know we Moloids will emerge, harm ground.

Surface dwellers, stay blind to what stirs beneath your feet.
Post your pathetic photos, ignore the mounting alarm ground.

We will fight back, pummel you with sticks and staffs, turn
the stink of your flowery towns a bloody Somme ground.

At last, the Invisible Woman will be mine. My Persephone,
immersed in the hollow earth, dare not resist my charm ground.

Shine now in the diamond's glare, my love, take the hand of Harvey
Rupert Elder, and this realm will be yours, a new Susan Storm ground.

TALES OF SUSPENSE #80

AUGUST 1966,
"HE WHO HOLDS THE COSMIC CUBE"

every atom belonging to me
as good belongs to you
—*Walt Whitman*

My mother says I was a breech birth
born feet-first as if, in the midst
of the *California Dreamin'*
Caped Crusader debut TV
screening, Vietnam War
protests, warp speed
launch of Star Trek,
birth of Miranda rights
and miniskirts zeitgeist,
on the sun-spliced morning
of August 10th, I leapt, like
the French mercenary Batroc,
directly into the breach.

That month, on the beach of his private Island
the Red Skull seizes control of the Cosmic
Cube. His new toy proves the greatest weapon
the world has ever known, a fist-sized Aladdin's
lamp with unlimited wishes. Captain America
bears witness when the Skull levitates a giant
boulder with the booming boast, *It displeases me!*
Let it defy gravity! Let it rise—until it is

out of sight! Stunned, Cap can only crouch
behind his shield, terrified by the realization,
With that cube in his hand, he has only to think
of something—and it happens! ... No longer
merely a dangerous foe ... this man who is
turning toward me now has become—invincible!

Oh, ye beseeching leapers, feet
frozen on the fringe of breaches—

shall we surrender so meekly?

Listen, I admit it, I'm the kind
of corny who needs a dang
scarecrow to defend the silky
stalks of my heart, who when
Cap says, *No matter how awe-*
some the odds—I'll never abandon
hope, feels those words resonate
like drums inside my throat.

Still, I don't eat Pollyanna-coated
flakes for breakfast. I damn sure
understand no matter how many
times Captain America splinters
his fire-shrieking cheekbone

The Red Skull will never perish.

Lest that gospel scare us, let us
also consider…if the Cosmic Cube
can make any wish tangible, then
it must somehow tentacle onto
even our brain molecules, must
somehow spark enough electricity
from our dreams to generate a chain,
as if our minds could hold hands
and construct a ring around the world
like the old Coca-Cola commercial

and sing loudly enough to render
any desire palpable.

Whitman says—

every atom in my marrow
swims in your blood too.

Lord, let that sentiment
be true, for if it is, can
we not hijack every
devious Red Skull
wish?

Are we not all our own Cosmic Cubes?

What, after all, is Marvel Comics
if not the sorcery of Lee holding
hands with the imaginations
of Kirby, Ditko, and all the other
pencil-pushing nerd-wizards?

What is the Marvel Universe
if not those buzzing visionaries
forming a grand chain that stretches
from the page through my brain,
and now, Good Reader, into yours?

Once more into the breach, my friends.

Feet first or head matters less
than whether we are willing,
one way or another, all our
treasured illusions already
shattered

to press forward
flex our calves

and leap.

OLD GUYS PLAYING SOFTBALL
ON MARTHA'S VINEYARD

*For Steve Rogers who makes the choice
to travel backward through time
so he can age through the seventy years
he missed*

The field, a treacherous moonscape—pockmarked
with bumps and fissures like some poor adolescent's
face, the twisting of ankles an expected casualty each
Sunday. Look, the ER's only 40 minutes away, and what
else would anyone have to do on a weekend afternoon?
Sit on the beach? You will or you won't, depends how
much that ankle swells, so, play ball, ya' bum, and keep
an eye out for the chasm in right-center. First pitch
is at eight in the morning, but in August, when the island's
stuffed with tourists, better get there by 7:30 or the game
starts without you.

Jerry, in the Mets jersey, knows this. He's been manning
the left side of the infield since before the advent of Spidey
despite sixteen knee surgeries. Don't test his arm on a ground
ball to short, or actually, do test it. He'd like nothing more
than to gun you out, Punisher-style, as you, thirty-year-old
with unscarred zest, bust it down the line to first.

All close plays are determined to be outs, but, in truth,
there aren't many close plays. Most balls lifted to the outfield
greet the uneven ground untouched and it's up to the batter,

or pinch-runner—who must start with one hand gripping
the backstop fence and cannot commence his journey
until the batter makes contact—to decide whether to stretch
the blooper into a double, which depends more than anything
on his own internal wind. No one slides—most players wear
shorts to show off their mangled knees and gnarled ankles—
and numerous outs occur due to overrunning the bag,
or, in a desperate attempt *not* to overrun the bag,
due to slowing down sufficiently so the throw
arrives at the base before the runner.

The competition is fierce. Teams are determined by everyone
throwing their gloves in a sloppy pile, and a daughter of a stalwart
who, thirty years ago, dove at least once per contest to snag a line-
drive over third and commit a grand theft, tosses one glove to the left,
one to the right, as if dividing the nation into political affiliations.

Wherever your glove lands,
whether it's a population
of Red Sox, Mets, or Yankees
fans, for today—

that's your team.

Score is kept by somebody's grandson on a rickety chalkboard
installed by a carpenter/first baseman decades ago, and you'd
best believe, if there's a mistake, if someone's run is forgotten,
that mistake will be rectified. *Every* run counts. I want to win.
I splash doubles that bounce in the rightfield gulch and try
to avoid overrunning second base. I tumble down a rabbit-
hole in leftfield and a can of corn drops to the ground in front
of me. Furious, I fire the ball toward the plate to nail the sept-
uagenarian runner but the octogenarian catcher watches the throw
sail over his head. Everybody scores and the grandson dutifully
marks the chalkboard. Somebody makes a joke about the ghost
of a former player, now dead.

When a teenager, some 56-year-old's son with muscles like Luke
Cage, launches a home run farther over the trees than has ever

previously been seen to salvage the win for my team, I am ecstatic.
My stumble and rainbow throw have not poisoned the hour.
The home run was hit off Fritz, an 85-year-old pitcher, who shrugs
when the ball can't be recovered from a garden of poison ivy and another
must be retrieved from the barrel. The final score is posted, then erased.
We promise to see each other next Sunday. We hope that promise
is kept.

ACKNOWLEDGMENTS

First things first, gratitude must be extended to the OGs—Stan Lee, Jack Kirby, Steve Ditko, Chris Claremont, Joe Simon, Frank Miller, Don McGregor, and any other Marvel writers who helped create the saga. Then, of course, the MCU peeps like Jon Favreau, Joss Whedon, James Gunn, Ryan Coogler, Anthony and Joe Russo, Taika Waititi, Sam Rami, Nicole Perlman, Kevin Feige for imagining it all, and any and all other personages who helped bring the stories from page to screen and gave them new vibrancy.

Special thanks to Steve Gillis for (true) believing in this book and for Michelle Dotter, Chelsea Gibbons, and everyone else at Dzanc for making it happen.

To poets who inspire me daily, including but not limited to the one and only Angel Nafis, Carlina Duan, Patricia Smith, Adam Falkner, Shira Erlichman, Aracelis Girmay, Noah Choi Wild, Aimeé Le, Sarah Kay, Danez Smith, Ross Gay, Franny Choi, Nate Marshall, José Olivarez, Kim Addonizio, Molly Raynor, Sonny Kennedy, Maggie Ambrosino, Lauren Whitehead, Hanif Abdurraquib, Dorianne Laux, Jim Daniels, Kevin Coval, Ellen Stone, Scott Beal, Patrick Rosal, Kaveh Akbar, Fiona Chamness, Brittany Rogers, Jon Sands, and Mahogany Browne.

Special shoutouts to Ray McDaniel and his collection *Special Powers and Abilities* and Marlin Jenkins and his collection *Capable*

Monsters for writing books that gave me permission to imagine mine. Better throw in Michael Chabon and *The Amazing Adventures of Kavalier & Clay* too.

Shoutout as well to the poet Teresa Scollon who first got me thinking about the importance of elegies.

To Douglas Wolk, whose *All the Marvels* helped me think about the larger shape of the Marvel story, and to Gavin Edwards, Dave Gonzales, and Joanna Robinson and their *MCU: The Reign of Marvel Studios*, which helped me affirm some of the important notes I was trying to hit, again, special thanks.

Gratitude to Adam Mansbach for the feedback, friendship, and encouragement.

Much love to all students past and present at Pioneer High School who listened to various versions of these poems in progress and, of course, to the Pioneer English Department and Don Packard, our own Cap, for assembling us and supporting all we do. Also to Pioneer's administration, including Principals Desmond Smith, Kevin Hudson, and Tracey Stevenson (plus past leaders Tracey Lowder, Jodi Bullinger, Dan Hyliard, and Jason Skiba) for more or less putting up with my shenanigans and supporting this work.

Love to the crew steering the ship over these past few months: Amy, Sonny, Peter, Paul, Karen, Molly, and Claire.

To the sibs Andy, Jim, Laura for always being there from the origin, and, of course, to Karen, Sam, and Julius for teaming up through all the adventures.

If we don't have belief each (and all) of us can save the world, what do we have?

ABOUT THE AUTHOR

Jeff Kass teaches tenth-grade English and Creative Writing in Ann Arbor MI. He's the award-winning author of *Knuckleheads*, Independent Publishers' Best Short Fiction Collection of 2011, as well as two full-length poetry collections, *My Beautiful Hook-nosed Beauty Queen Strut Wave* and *Teacher/Pizza Guy*, a 2020 Michigan Notable Book. He has taught poetry classes and workshops to thousands of students and is a recipient of a prestigious 2023 Jack Hazard Fellowship for writers who teach in public schools.